ANIMAL SAFARI

Polar Bears

by Kari Schuetz

BLASTOFF! READERS

BELLWETHER MEDIA · MINNEAPOLIS, MN

Note to Librarians, Teachers, and Parents:

Blastoff! Readers are carefully developed by literacy experts and combine standards-based content with developmentally appropriate text.

Level 1 provides the most support through repetition of high-frequency words, light text, predictable sentence patterns, and strong visual support.

Level 2 offers early readers a bit more challenge through varied simple sentences, increased text load, and less repetition of high-frequency words.

Level 3 advances early-fluent readers toward fluency through increased text and concept load, less reliance on visuals, longer sentences, and more literary language.

Level 4 builds reading stamina by providing more text per page, increased use of punctuation, greater variation in sentence patterns, and increasingly challenging vocabulary.

Level 5 encourages children to move from "learning to read" to "reading to learn" by providing even more text, varied writing styles, and less familiar topics.

Whichever book is right for your reader, Blastoff! Readers are the perfect books to build confidence and encourage a love of reading that will last a lifetime!

This edition first published in 2012 by Bellwether Media, Inc.

No part of this publication may be reproduced in whole or in part without written permission of the publisher. For information regarding permission, write to Bellwether Media, Inc., Attention: Permissions Department, 5357 Penn Avenue South, Minneapolis, MN 55419.

Library of Congress Cataloging-in-Publication Data
Schuetz, Kari.
  Polar bears / by Kari Schuetz.
    p. cm. – (Blastoff! readers. animal safari)
  Includes bibliographical references and index.
  Summary: "Developed by literacy experts for students in kindergarten through grade three, this book introduces polar bears to young readers through leveled text and related photos"–Provided by publisher.
  ISBN 978-1-60014-609-1 (hardcover : alk. paper)
  1. Polar bear–Juvenile literature. I. Title.
  QL737.C27S38 2012
  599.786–dc22   2011008190

Text copyright © 2012 by Bellwether Media, Inc. BLASTOFF! READERS and associated logos are trademarks and/or registered trademarks of Bellwether Media, Inc. SCHOLASTIC, CHILDREN'S PRESS, and associated logos are trademarks and/or registered trademarks of Scholastic Inc.

Printed in the United States of America, North Mankato, MN.

080111   1187

Contents

What Are Polar Bears?

Polar bears are the largest kind of bear in the world.

Polar bears live in the **Arctic**. They blend in with ice and snow.

Paws, Fur, and Blubber

Polar bears have rough pads on their paws. The pads keep polar bears steady on ice.

pads

Thick fur and
fat keep polar
bears warm.
Their fat is
called **blubber**.

Swimming and Playing

Blubber also helps polar bears float. They are good swimmers.

Polar bears paddle with their front paws. They use their back paws to **steer**.

Polar bears often play-fight. They move their heads back and forth when they want to play!

Hunting

Polar bears are **predators**. They hunt seals and other **prey**.

Polar bears wait near water for prey to come up for air. Then they attack!

Glossary

Arctic—the cold, northern part of the world

blubber—fat; polar bears have blubber under their fur.

predators—animals that hunt other animals for food

prey—animals that are hunted by other animals for food

steer—to direct movement

To Learn More

AT THE LIBRARY

Baek, Matthew J. *Panda & Polar Bear.* New York, N.Y.: Dial Books for Young Readers, 2009.

Kalman, Bobbie. *Baby Polar Bears.* New York, N.Y.: Crabtree Pub. Co., 2011.

Shively, Julie D. *Baby Polar Bear.* Nashville, Tenn.: CandyCane Press, 2005.

ON THE WEB

Learning more about polar bears is as easy as 1, 2, 3.

1. Go to www.factsurfer.com.

2. Enter "polar bears" into the search box.

3. Click the "Surf" button and you will see a list of related Web sites.

With factsurfer.com, finding more information is just a click away.

Index

The images in this book are reproduced through the courtesy of: Peter Kirillov, front cover, p. 5; John Foster / Masterfile, p. 7; Steven Kazlowski / Photolibrary, p. 9 (top); Daniel Cox / Photolibrary, p. 9 (bottom); Henry Wilson, p. 11; Olga Ershova, p. 13; Henrik Winther Anderson, p. 15; Florida Stock, p. 17; Alaska Stock / Photolibrary, p. 19; Andy Gehrig, p. 21.